Eating the flesh of other people conveys strength, speed, immortality, and a nasty streak a mile wide. A wendigo can hibernate for years, then come out of it and hunt. They'll keep their victims alive and feed off them for a while.

Bullets won't stop them, and they're impervious to knives, too. Fire's the only thing that'll work.

SUPERNATURAL

JOIN THE HUNT

THIS BELONGS TO

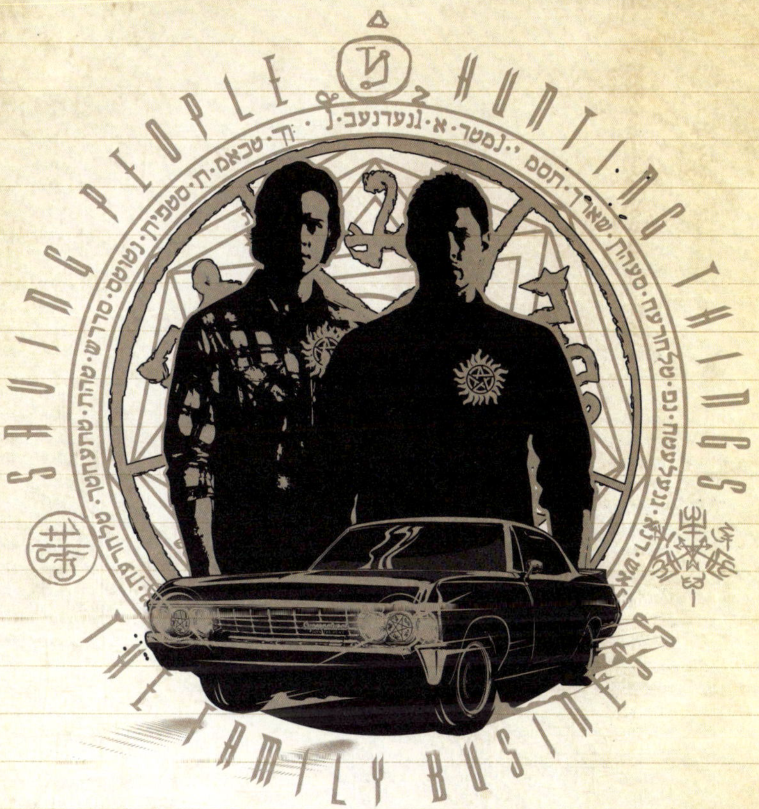

SUPERNATURAL
JOIN THE HUNT

INSIGHTS
www.insighteditions.com

MANUFACTURED IN CHINA
10 9 8 7 6 5 4 3 2 1

The vetala comes from Hindu mythology. It's a creature that looks beautiful on the outside but is pure evil on the inside. They capture their prey and feed on their blood, usually for several days at a time.

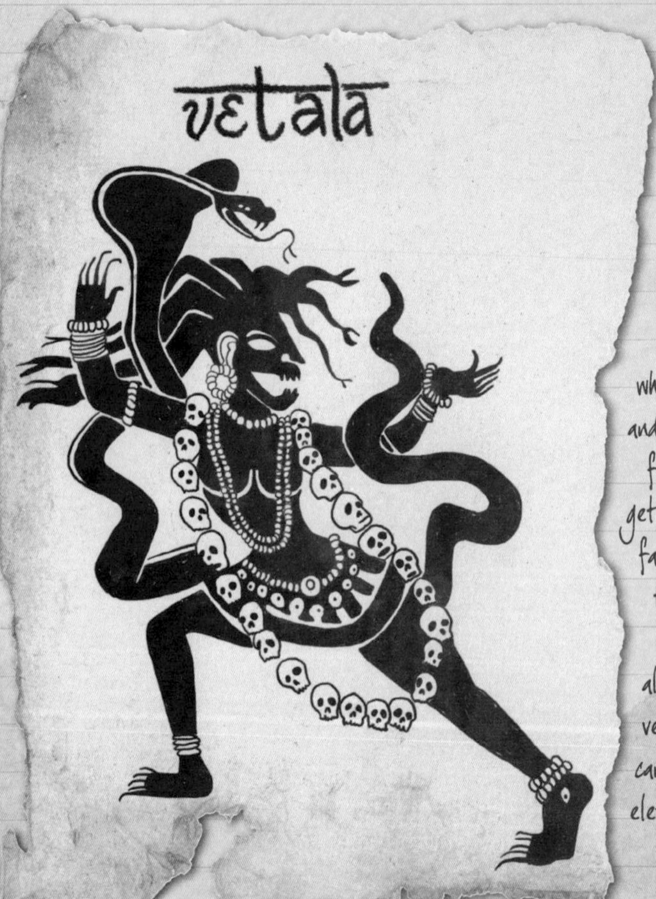

When they look human, they tend toward looking all pretty, but then their real form comes out when they attack and when they feed. Their eyes get white, their fangs grow, and they start to feed. Their fangs also secrete a venom that can put down an elephant.

There's only one way to kill them. guns and knives will hurt them, but they heal pretty fast. You need a silver knife, stab them in the heart with it, then twist it once. After the twist, they're permanently dead and will turn to dust.